Recovery

More Than One Day At A Time

Other Books By Rhonda Skinner Sullivan:

- **Thou Shalt Not Abuse Thy Spouse**
- **Mind of A Whore:** The Quest To Save The Christian Family
- **Christ in the Workplace:** The Employee Handbook

Recovery: More Than One Day At A Time

Printed in the United States of America
©2006 by Rhonda Skinner Sullivan
All Rights Reserved.

Library of Congress cataloged
ISBN: 0-9788545-3-5

We Family Ministries
P.O. Box 40644
Jacksonville, FL 32211

For prayer requests or praise reports, please e-mail us at: wefamily904@aol.com

No part of this book may be reproduced or transmitted in any form or by any means, electronic or mechanical, including photocopying, recording, or by any information and retrieval system, without permission in writing from the author or publisher.

To facilitate understanding and correlation to modern

Dedication

To Tyrone, Jezsika, and Ta' Mera
You are my twelve step recovery program.
Thank you for helping me to heal, not from addiction but from abuse.
You are truly angels on earth because I know that healing and restoration comes from God and he used you for this purpose in my life.

I LOVE YOU ALL!!

Table of Contents

5	**INTRODUCTION TO THE PROGRAM**		
6	**INVITATION OF LIVE**		

STEPS

7	ONE	Identify Your Idol
12	TWO	Claim Your Inheritance
16	THREE	Put Away The Double-Edged Sword
20	FOUR	Repent
23	FIVE	Pour Out The Poison
26	SIX	Free Yourself
31	**FASTING CREED**	
32	SEVEN	Do The Good You Ought To Do
37	EIGHT	Renew Your Mind
40	**AFFIRMATION**	
41	NINE	Reclaim You Inheritance
44	TEN	Live More Than One Day At A Time
50	ELEVEN	Walk By Faith Not By Sight
56	TWELVE	Share Your Blessing
58	**IN ALL THINGS GIVE PRAISE**	
59	**EVERDAY BATTLE PRAYERS**	

Introduction to the Program

Addiction of any kind but especially substance abuse is a sin that ravages health, financial resources, families, and life, in general. It draws you away from everything good into a life of pain, despair, and death. Many rehabilitation programs offer a 12 step program for recovery. The success rate varies but none of them offer a 100% success rate.

If this unsuccessful success rate frustrates you, do not give up, give in. Jesus offers a rehabilitation program that has a 100% success rate. He is the answer for those attempting to overcome addiction for the first time as well as those who have relapsed under secular drug and alcohol treatment models. He provides a permanent solution for recovery from addiction.

Your past failures do not have to be your future. Don't let Satan deceive you by telling you that you have little or no control over your actions or that you are doomed to a life of sickness, poverty, or death. Your destiny is not a lifetime of relapse, therapy, and meetings. This is neither God's truth nor His plan for your life. One day at a time is not enough! Jesus offers you life an abundant and prosperous, eternal life.

Invitation to Live

Welcome to Righteous Recovery where our motto is, "Recovery Is More Than One Day At A Time". We offer a 12 step program that guarantees you success in overcoming your addiction. Our 100% success rate gives you life not only for today and tomorrow but for eternity.

Righteous Recovery offers:
- Unlimited 24 hour one on one care, intervention, and counseling
- Family support
- Addiction education
- Peer groups
- Detoxification
- "**Holy**istic" treatment encompassing mental, physical, emotional, and spiritual healing

The owner and overseer, Jesus Christ, and I are glad that you have chosen to take your life back from the enemy. You will be transformed and restored!

Step 1

Identify Your Idol

You shall have no other gods before me.
Exodus 20:3

Millions of Americans get hooked on drugs like heroin, morphine, tranquilizers, and cocaine every year but the reach of addiction stretches much farther. It includes nicotine, caffeine, diets, sugar, steroids, work, theft, gambling, exercise, sex, and anything else you put before God. Addiction is a sin. It is idolatry and is the leading cause of death for unrepentant believers. It destroys human beings on every level of existence. It ravages them mentally, physically, emotionally, and especially spiritually. Addiction leaves the addict drowning in a sea of loneliness, failure, and despair. Some addicts never come to know the Lord as they are blinded by Satan's lies. Others are drawn away from Him in their continuous quests to find refuge from the pain. Unfortunately for most, without deliverance, they will resign themselves to their addiction and to death. The wages of sin is death. (Romans 6:23)

Almost all addicts tell themselves that they can quit on their own. Unfortunately, this is not the case. You can do nothing without God.(Romans 11:36). Successful recovery requires a greater power and that power lies in salvation through Christ Jesus. Recovery demands that you go through a process of being transformed to be more and more like the image of God. Jesus came to save the sinner "completely". (Hebrews 7:25). All you have to do is receive Him.
Addiction is the manifestation of some thirst that needs to be quenched or a physical pain that needs to

be numbed.

Addicts try to quench that thirst with everything but God. But only Jesus can quench your thirst. This is why the "one day at a time" philosophy of secular rehabilitation programs is so ineffective. It draws the addict away from God to the mirage of carnal healing from a spiritual illness.

Deliverance from addiction requires supernatural provision. No matter what you are addicted to, Jesus offers hope. He offers so much more than "one day at a time" for the believer who repents, is forgiven, and chooses to walk in obedience to God's Word. He offers eternal life. Whoever eats of the living bread will live forever.(John 6:51)

Successful recovery is a multi-phase, multi-faceted, life-long process. Physical detoxification alone is not sufficient. There needs to be a spiritual detoxification. This spiritual detoxification will equip you with new tools to deal with temptation, trials, set-backs, and life in general. First, you <u>must</u> make a decision to have no other god before the Heavenly Father. This commitment will propel you into a place of freedom from the undertow of addiction.

Who's <u>Your</u> Idol?

For our struggle is not against flesh and blood, but against the rulers, against the authorities, against the powers of this dark world and against the spiritual forces of evil in the heavenly realms.
Ephesians 6:12

Matthew 6:24 says that you cannot serve two masters. You must chose which master you want to serve, Satan who offers you addiction, destruction, and death or Jesus who offers deliverance, restoration, and life. Recovery requires that you realize that the idol you are worshiping is an evil spirit or spirits. These demons enter through doors left open by sin in your life. Sin must be rebuked. If Satan is talking to you, do not listen to him.(1 Timothy 5:20) The devil cannot defeat you if you don't give in. Stand firm in your faith and the authority you have in Jesus' name. Don't accept defeat! God's word provides all the answers.

Victory over addiction requires embracing the truth and staying committed to God. To be purged from this life of sin and destruction, allow a mighty move of God to occur in your life. Receive deliverance through confession of your sin. Hate unrighteousness as much as God does. Stand firm on your faith. Make your life a life of daily worship, prayer, and obedience. Study the Word. It will bring the knowledge and wisdom that will sustain you through your trial. Be vigilant in your spiritual warfare. Recognize Satan's devices and utilize God-given authority over all the powers of darkness. We are called to be soldiers and to stand firmly in obedience to the Word of God. Be prepared to do battle for your deliverance, recovery, and restoration.

Satan is the author of lies. He will distort the truth so that your shortcomings will blind you of the love and forgiveness of God. He ignites distrust to cause you to alienate yourself from other believers and from God. Satan will use any means necessary to keep you from acknowledging God's authority over your life.

Addiction is a life or death game that can only be won with God as the captain of your team. His Word is your game-plan. Take an offensive approach to Satan's attempts. Satan will try to set a trap for you or put stumbling blocks in your path to impede your progress for God. He will entice you to sin. Victory over his deception requires that you remember that we are all imperfect. You will continually struggle against inadequacy and limitations as long as you live in your earthly body. When you fall short of His glory by allowing some sin to enter your life, stand firm on God's faithfulness to forgive you and His desire for you to live.

Victory over addiction and Satan's attempts to draw you into sin and condemnation requires a strategic approach. His faultfinding demons seek to hinder if not halt your
progress in God. Acknowledge your shortcomings in that area and reassure Satan that God knows all about it. Tell him that God loves you anyway, has forgiven you, and will help you to rise above the sin in your life. Proclaim God's faithfulness, righteousness, and glory so that Satan knows that he has no power in your life.

MY TRANSFORMATION

___
___
___
___

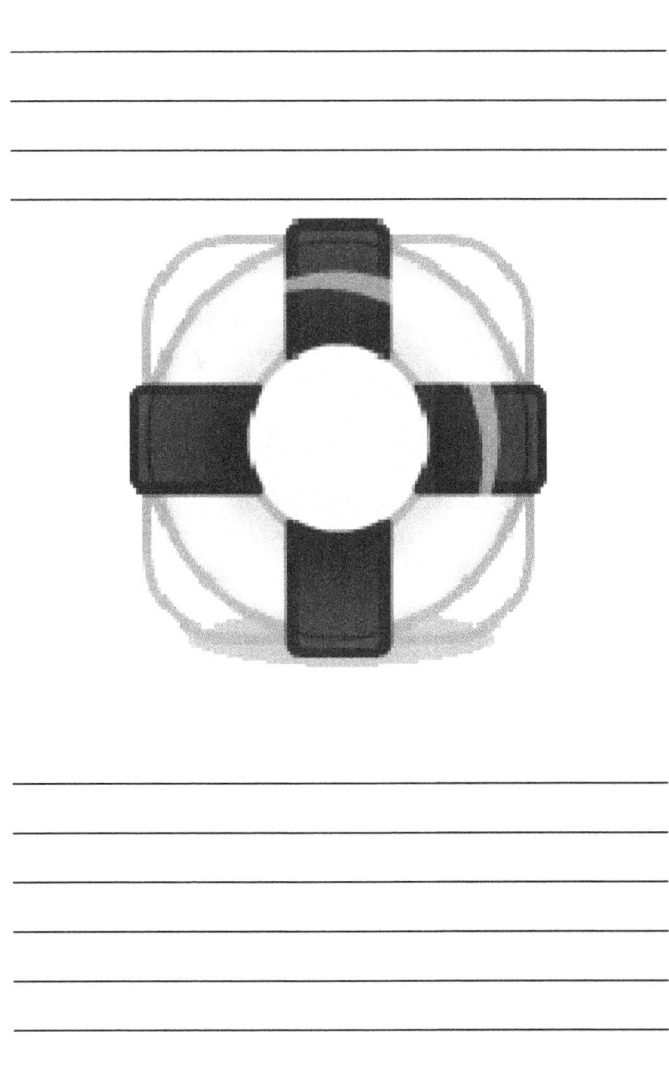

___
___
___
___
___
___
___

STEP 2

Claim Your Inheritance

It was not through law that Abraham and his offspring received the promise that he would be heir of the world, but through the righteousness that comes by faith.
Romans 4:13

The next step towards recovery is to make a conscious choice to live. It means realizing that you can do nothing without Jesus, yet all things through Him. (Philippians 4:13) He will provide everything you need to recover from whatever binds you. He is your rock, your fortress, your shield, your deliverer. He offers you refuge.(Psalm 18:2) He is your stronghold in times of trouble.(Psalm 37:39)

First you must accept Him into your heart and allow Him to be master over every part of you. If you do not know the Lord or have been drawn away from Him by a life of sin, you must reclaim your inheritance. Pray the following prayer in faith and you will be saved.

Father God,

Today I confess that I am a sinner. I believe that Jesus Christ died for my sins and that I am justified through His resurrection. I confess Him as my personal savior right now and receive Him into my heart to transform me into all that God has called me to be.

In the Jesus name...Amen

The new birth is the foundation for recovery. It opens the door for the removal of sin and the reward of eternal life. Jesus is the way and the truth and the life. No one comes to the Father except through Him. (John 14:6)

As a new or reborn believer, you are entitled to the rights of the King. God appointed you to receive salvation, not to suffer wrath.(1 Thessalonians 5:9) Salvation will equip you with the necessary tools to achieve successful recovery from addiction. With salvation comes the grace of God.(Titus 2:11) and the favor of God which will help you through the trials of life.(Isaiah 49:8) Salvation brings ministering angels who are sent to serve you with protection, wisdom, and guidance.(Hebrews 1:14) It offers you joy. (Isaiah 12:3)

Once you have chosen to serve God, you must humble yourself to His power for the necessary transformation to occur. Successful recovery requires that you regain control over your life through submission to God. Ultimately, everyone must submit to authority.(Romans 13:1) Submission to God resists the devil and causes him to flee.(James 4:7) It offers peace and prosperity.(Job 22:21)

Never forget the sacrifice He made for you. He was forsaken so that you do not have to be. He paid the penalty for every one of your sins. He died a criminal's death so that you will have a king's life. He suffered shame and disgrace so that you don't have to. His condemnation redeemed you. Addiction negates everything that God did for you. It keeps you held up in the same pit of hell that Jesus delivered you from. Take hold of His truth. Let love, forgiveness, and obedience guide your life. He will light your path to recovery with whatever you need. Ask him to reveal your sin and give thanks for deliverance. Declare your dependence on Jesus and victory over the Devil. Acknowledge Jesus' power over you as your friend, your Savior, your protector, your Lord.

MY TRANSFORMATION

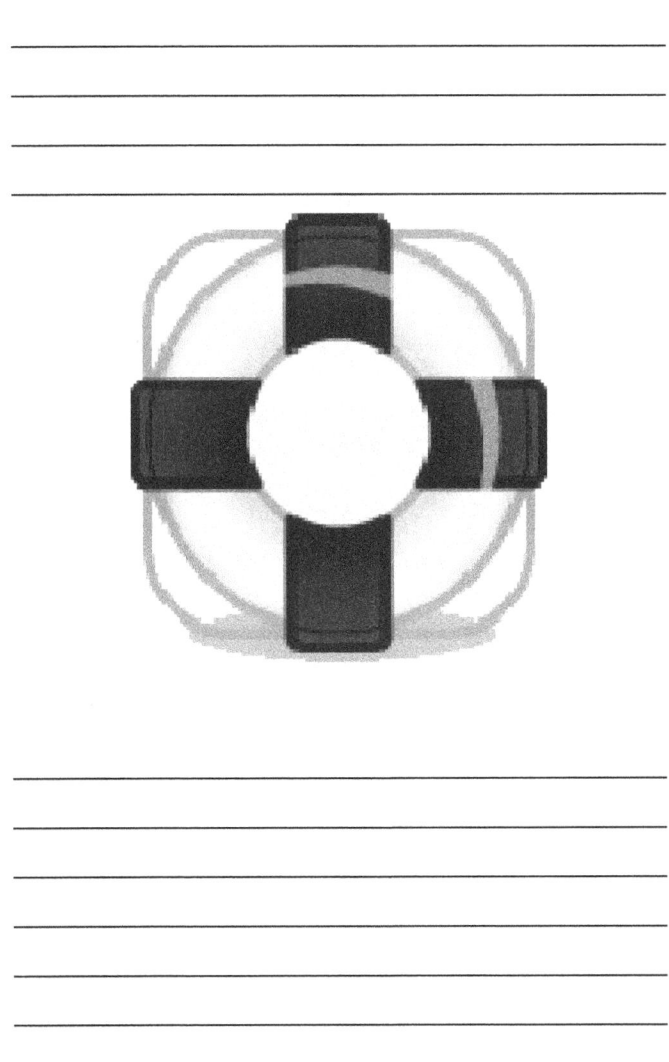

STEP 3

The Double-Edged Sword

> He who guards his lips guards his life, but he who speaks rashly will come to ruin.
> **Proverbs 13:3**

Ten of the twelve curses that came upon the children of Israel in the wilderness were caused by murmuring. Instead of murmuring and complaining, the Word tells us to rejoice and give thanks always. The next step to recovery, lies in your words. First and foremost, they make salvation a reality. If you confess with your mouth that "Jesus is Lord," and believe in your heart that God raised Him from the dead, you will be saved.(Romans 10:9) Words release our faith. Our words call those things that are not as though they are.(Romans 4:17) We have a voice in heaven. Our words petition the Lord for His help, His wisdom, and His refuge.

Mark 16:20 tells us that as you speak Godly things He will confirm your words with signs. He will make our requests a reality. Words open spiritual doors that allow us to exercise our spiritual authority. Jesus used words to heal the sick, cast out evil spirits, raise the dead, and to calm the storm. Right words summon the glory of the Lord. Addiction, a spirit, flees in its presence.

Words summon forgiveness and allow you to operate in the love of God. Since addiction is often the manifestation of unresolved pain, recovery requires letting go of the pain and reaching for God's provision. He will heal you physically, emotionally, and spiritually so that you can be all that He has called you to be. 1 John 1:9 says that if you confess your sins that God is faithful and just to forgive you and cleanse us from all unrighteousness, even addiction. The power of life and death is in your tongue.(Proverbs 18:21) You can please or displease God with what you speak over your life. Words control your thoughts and direct your actions. Your thoughts and your actions will listen to what you say. If you speak life over your situation then you will have life. On the other hand, if you speak negativity, destruction, and death over your circumstances then you will have the same.

Avoid negative confessions. Murmuring and complaining give the devil the advantage. Remember that you have a loving, faithful, all-powerful Father watching over you. Show Him that you believe His Word and will stand in faith on His promises for your deliverance, peace, and restoration. Confess who God is and what His word says you are. Be swift to hear and slow to speak. (James 1:19) To have life, you must speak life into your circumstances. Pessimism is of the devil. Proverbs 10:21 says that righteous lips can feed many. Your words have the ability to impact your life and the lives of others around you. Learn to say good things about yourself and others. The Word says that your words show what is in your heart.(Matthew 12:34) What comes out of your mouth will define you.(Matthew 15:11) Choose life and receive forgiveness by speaking the truth; not your truth but God's truth.

Confess your sin in obedience to the Word. Declare your future. God's word tells you who you are and what you will become. Tell the devil what God has done for you. Confess his control over your life and Satan's powerlessness to change that. Confess your desire to walk in obedience to God's word. Encourage yourself in God, knowing that God is faithful. He is not a man that He should lie.(Numbers 29:13) He will do what He says He will do. Confession offers hope for the future, not just for today, but for eternity.

MY TRANSFORMATION

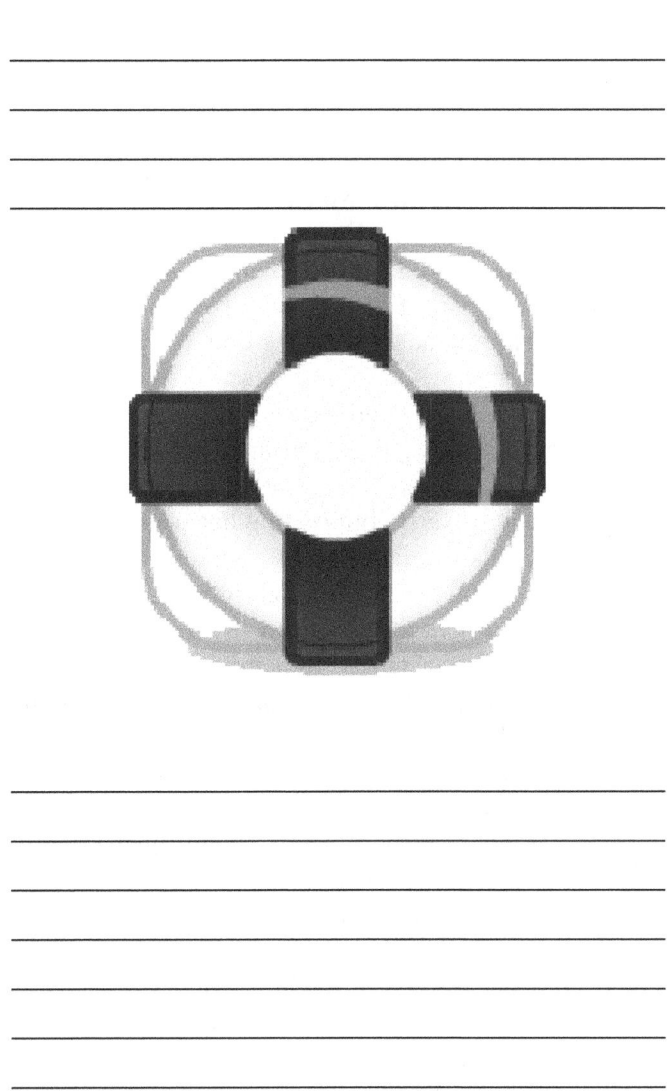

STEP 4

Repent

> There will be more rejoicing in heaven over one sinner who repents than ninety-nine righteous people who do not need to repent.
> **Luke 15:17**

Repentance is yielding to Jesus and giving Him ownership over your life. Matthew 6:24 says that you cannot serve to masters. Repentance is changing masters from Satan to God. It is allowing Jesus to be Lord over every aspect of your life. It separates you from the world and acknowledges that your sin was killed on Calvary.

Godly sorrow brings repentance and leaves no regret.(2 Corinthians 7:10) Repentance brings rest. (Isaiah 30:15) Leviticus 5:5 says that anyone who is guilty in any way must confess in what way he has sinned. Sin is disobedience and separates you from God. It causes spiritual death. Sin ignores the sacrifice of Jesus and says to him that you do not love Him nor appreciate His sacrifice. Repentance says that you recognize His sacrifice and are committed to repaying Him with obedience.

Recovery, a spiritual change, starts from the inside out. Repentance is the key. Repentance comes from the heart. It takes the power away from the devil and frees your will for God to control your life. It changes the way you think.(Isaiah 30:15) This changes your actions so that they become more Christ-like.

Once sin occurs, a return to righteousness requires a heartfelt confession and repentance. You must believe and trust Him to do what His word says He will do and then act in obedience. Without this you are doomed. Matthew 7:21-23 says that at the day of judgment, God will rebuke those who work iniquity. He will profess to have never known them. You must forsake the world of sin to be worthy of the kingdom. No matter how your life fails, God knows your path. He is continuously molding you and leading in the direction that He has for your life. He has made provision for your sin. There is no sin too great for Him to remove from your life.

Maintaining progress in recovery requires continuously taking personal inventory, and when you are wrong, promptly admitted it. He will blot out your transgressions and remember your sins no more. (Isaiah 43:25) Accept your forgiveness. It is always there but you have to claim it by freeing your will in confession and repentance.

MY TRANSFORMATION

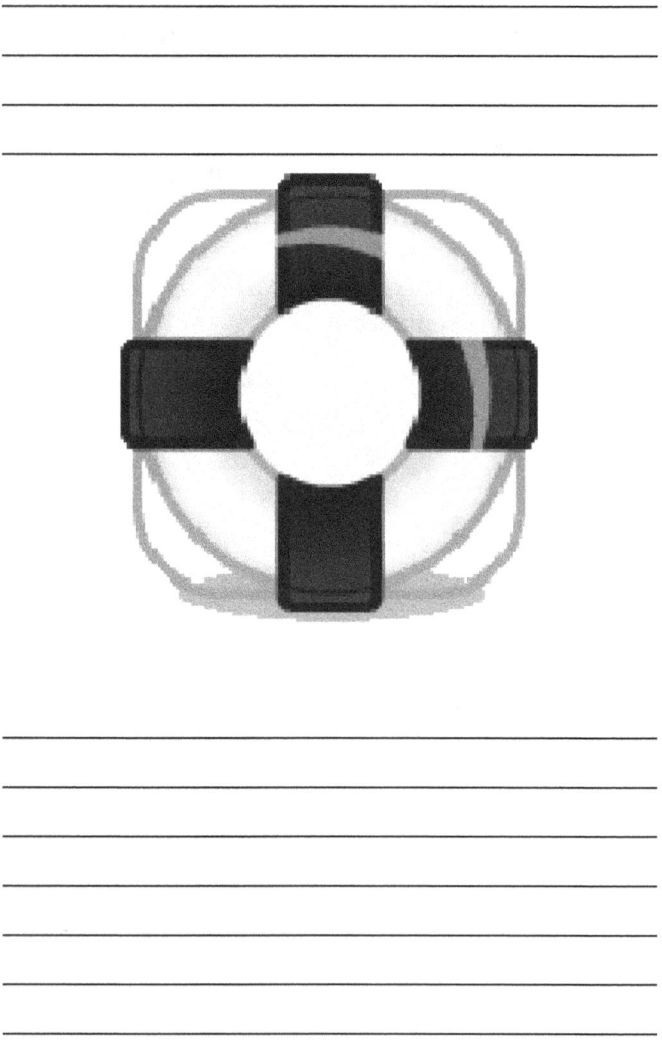

STEP 5

Pouring Out the Poison

> For if you forgive men when they sin
> against you, your heavenly Father will also
> forgive you.
> **Matthew 6:14**

Several things can result in addictive behaviors. Early childhood trauma, like sexual or physical abuse can lead people to seek refuge in addiction. Learning disabilities, attention deficit disorder, schizophrenia, and depression can lead a person to find solace in addiction. Regardless of what your past pain is, leaving these issues unresolved can lead to unforgiveness, bitterness, discouragement, depression, and other sin. Addiction is simply a cover-up for these sinful feelings. For many, it provides an escape from the pain. What many do not realize is that the relief lasts only as long as the high lasts.

Addiction brings on a spirit of heaviness that binds you. It drains you of the courage and the persistence to run the race. It distorts your thinking and makes the hope of recovery appear unrealistic. It dims God's light with worry, fear, disinterest, failure, inadequacy, and hopelessness. These emotions are sin. They permit the devil to override your knowledge of God's Word and give him permission to operate in your mind and in your heart. Satan will take whatever power you give him and use it for your destruction. Overcoming Satan requires that you remember who he is and recognize his devices. Satan is the adversary, the deceiver, and the accuser. There is nothing good in him. He comes to steal, kill, and destroy.

Addiction is one of these subtle devices that

occasionally manifest itself as a "harmless habit". Some addictions, because they do not cause a noticeable harm, may sneak up on you. Many do not see its destruction until it is too late. This again, is a device of the deceiver, Satan. Ignorance to the enemy's devices, even subtle ones, can hinder God's work in you. Ignorance allows you to verbally forgive someone while holding unforgiveness in your heart toward that person. It tells you to accept condemnation as a way of life. Ignorance makes you accept a failed recovery as your destiny. Don't accept these lies as your truth. Exercise your authority and stop Satan from hindering God's plan for your life. God has forgiven you and you must forgive yourself. His Word requires it.

No matter what you are addicted to, "anonymous" does not work. Confession is the only way to restoration. If we confess our sins, he is faithful and just and will forgive us our sins and purify us from all unrighteousness.(1John 1:9) Therefore confess your sins to each other and pray for each other so that you may be healed.(James 5:16) God's forgiveness offers true deliverance. It offers hope. Choose to be a steward over your mind. Free your will and allow God to forgive you. Take away Satan's power in your life by releasing your past and grabbing hold of your future.

MY TRANSFORMATION

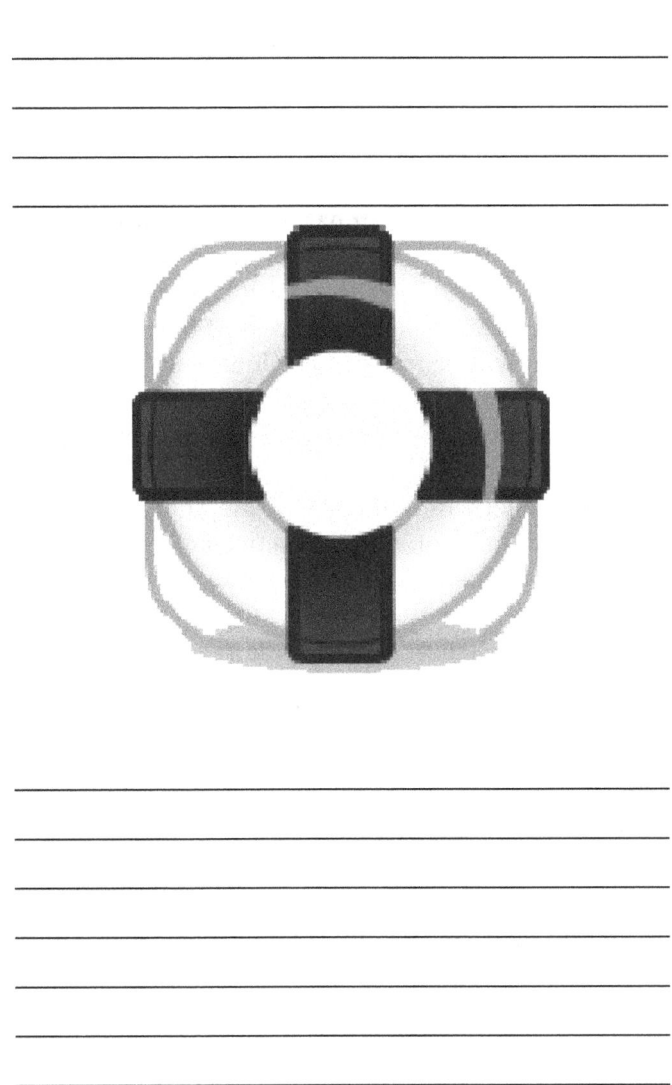

STEP 6

Free Yourself

> Yes, and I will continue to rejoice, for I know that through your prayers and the help given by the Spirit of Jesus Christ, what has happened to me will turn out for my deliverance.
> **Philippians 1:19**

Addiction brings condemnation which is a spirit of guilt. Condemnation comes from the devil. Recovery requires deliverance from this spirit of shame. Deliverance comes from God.(Psalm 3:8) If the son sets you free, you will be free indeed.(John 8:36) Jesus will set you free by answering the pain in your life. He will give you the power through Jesus to overcome the temptations of addiction.

Recovery offers an immediate feeling of success and accomplishment. You will feel better and do better in every aspect of life. Even when struggles come and they will, face them with Godly perseverance. God offers a life of freedom, dignity, and restoration.

Mark 21:22 says that if you ask and do not doubt what you ask, it will be done. Deliverance from the spirit of addiction and its accompanying spirit of condemnation requires that you simply ask and believe in faith that it is yours. Accept freedom as your gift. Jesus says, "For where two or three come together in my name, there am I with them.". (Matthew 18:20) If you do not have the faith to call your deliverance into existence, seek the help of other believers who can pray for you and agree in prayer for your deliverance.

Recovery requires that you release the sin and condemnation and receive the deliverance that God has for you. Know that you are forgiven because the word of God tells you are. After your deliverance, you must fill your spirit with the Word. Matthew 12:44-46 says that evil spirits will return to their house seeking refuge. When it arrives, if it finds the house unoccupied, swept clean and put in order or devoid of God's Word, then it goes and takes with it seven other spirits more wicked than itself, and they go in and live there. Maintaining deliverance requires that you substitute the substance in the Word for sin. If not, the Word promises that your final condition will be worse than before.

No matter how bad things get, don't run away from God. Run to Him. He loves you and will help you to rise above your situation. You are redeemed by His sacrifice and nothing you do can change that. Accept His love, forgiveness, and deliverance. It is yours!

As you release the sin, you will find that the enemy will bring all types of lies to you to tell you that you cannot succeed. Some of his devices will be the façade of cravings and withdrawals. But his words are just that, lies. One way to deter his attempts at causing you to relapse includes a purification process, caused fasting. It is a privilege of believers and not only necessary but scriptural.

Fasting, abstaining from food for the purpose of seeking God, has many benefits. Fasting tells God that you desire Him more than anything else. It reveals the heart of God to offer supernatural provision for your needs. It disciplines your spirit and controls your body so that you will gain victory in Satan's attacks. It breaks the hold of demonic forces in your life, like drugs, alcohol, sex, or any other addiction. Fasting brings God's anointing over your life into focus and removes distractions. It humbles you. It reduces your power so that the power of the Holy Spirit can work more intensely within you for your success. Fasting offers you an inner peace that will sustain you. Fasting offers freedom from discouragement, desolation, failure, pain, and suffering. Your heavy burdens will be lifted. Fasting helps you to rise above obscurity into the place of honor that God has for you. You will gain self-control through renewed spiritual vision and a determination to follow God's plan for your life.

2 Corinthians 7 tells you to cleanse yourself from 'all' filthiness of the flesh and spirit, so that you can receive the promises of God. Addiction is filthy not only because it results in harmful toxins being put into God's temple of the Holy Spirit, your body, but because it opens the door for other sin like sexual impurity, lying, gluttony, and stealing to name a few.

In recovery, fasting offers both a spiritual and physical purification. Supernatural purification of your body comes as you submit your mind and body to the Holy Spirit. Additionally, as you abstain your body will be purified of many harmful toxins found in the food you eat everyday. Committing to obedience will help you to recognize the cravings that attempt to draw you back to addiction as sin. God will take them away. Other physical and emotional signs of withdrawal like shaking, nervousness, anxiety, and anger will stop as you focus on the love of God and His purpose for your life.

Fasting requires meditating on the Word. The Word fills the space previously occupied by your addiction and helps you to remember God's mandates for your life. These are the same commands that tell you that addiction and abuse is idolatry. They are sins that lead to death. Commit yourself to a fasted life free of all of the things that seek to destroy your body, mind, and soul.

Once you have chosen to fast, you must decide on a type of fast. There are two categories of fasts. Fasts can be proclaimed or public which encompasses participation from a church, a city, or a nation. Proclaimed fast, also known as corporate fast create unity and direct your attention to a shared concern. Personal fast are declared by the Holy Spirit or by the believer who wants to establish a more intimate relationship with God. There are two major types of fast. A total fast requires that you avoid eating all food for a period of time. It does allow you to drink water. A partial fast requires that you abstain from one food or substance for a period of time. A partial fast may also include not over-eating.(Luke 21:34 and Philippians 3:19) Partial fast do not allow you to eat desserts or other delicacies.(Daniel 10:3)

When you fast, remember that it is a strategic counter-attack on Satan. First declare the purpose of your fast and speak to deliverance from a spirit of addiction. Proclaim the fast before the Lord. Claim your deliverance, healing, and restoration in faith. Study the Word to fill your spirit with spiritual food. Stay in prayer. Trust God to do what His Word says He will do. He will!

MY TRANSFORMATION

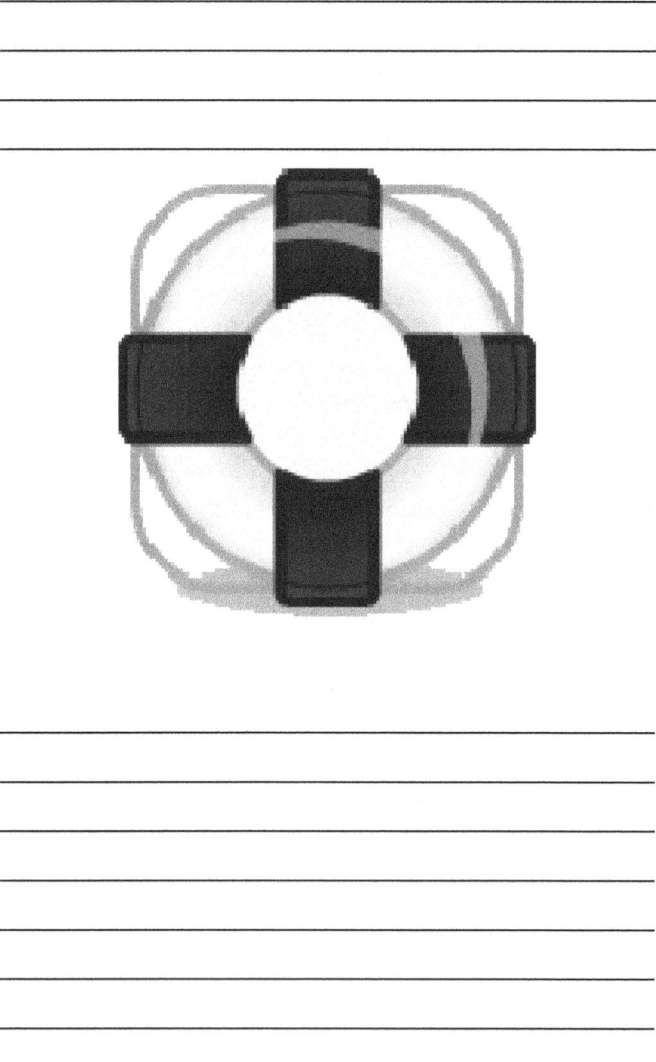

The fasting creed will help you to track your fasts. It will reveal the faithfulness of God to honor your obedience.

Fasting Creed

Dates of Fast:_____

Father God,

I am fasting for (reason/s) _____.

I will abstain from (food/meal) _____ for (time)_____.

I will focus my bible study on (scripture/topics)
_____
_____
_____
_____

In Jesus' Name, Amen

BREAKTHROUGH NOTES:
_____
_____
_____
_____
_____
_____
_____
_____

Step 7

The Good You Ought To Do

He sent forth his word and healed them; he rescued them from the grave.
Psalm 107:20

You must meditate on the Word daily to successfully overcome your addiction. God has set before all believers specific guidelines for receiving the abundant life promised in His word. The Word will change your life. It will renew your thinking, build faith, and bring the blessings of God into your life. Obedience to it is the only way to receive your Godly inheritance. God's word keeps the devil under your feet by exposing his lies and your power over him. God's word offers prophetic confirmation and feeds your spirit. It saves souls and changes destinies.

Your will is developed through meditation on the Word. It will eventually give in to God as you grow in love and obedience to Christ. God's word is a magnifying glass. It allows you to see yourself the way God sees you; blameless, forgiven, and righteous.

Jesus is righteous. Because He lives in you, you are righteous. Recovery means never forgetting your place of righteousness. The enemy will seek to fill your head with condemnation and lies. Learning God's word will teach you to resist the devil in thought, word, and action.

Desire the sincere milk of the word.(1 Peter 2:2) This milk is necessary for spiritual growth. Feed your spirit daily. When you study the Word, ask the Lord to reveal Himself to you. Expect God to speak to you. Train your spirit to hear from God through an intimacy with Him. He is ready to forgive you and change your life.

Read His Word with optimism. Avoid allowing the enemy to condemn you because of your shortcomings. The Word will correct you by revealing the areas of change for your life. Separate yourself from the distractions of life. Don't allow Satan to make you lazy or disinterested during your studies. Meditate on what you read and search for its application to your life. Receive the Word and put your confidence in it by faith. His word will develop and perfect you. When the trials of addiction, sickness, and sin come your way; run to the Word. It offers answers and will equip you for the battle ahead of you. Hide the Word in your heart.(Psalm 119:11) Overcome sin and the author of sin the same way Jesus did, with the Word.

In this modern age of technology there are many ways to feed your spirit. Many teachings are available on tape, compact disc, and DVD. Many of these teachings are spirit lead and serve the purpose of enriching your life. Forsake not the assembling of the saints. Many churches provide different methods of learning, as well. But don't give in to complacency with regard to church service. Remember to stay focused and to come with an expectancy to hear from the heart of God. Reading different translations may also prevent complacency. Quiet time with God's Word is just as important. It builds intimacy and offers comfort and strength. Watching ministers on television also provides another venue for sowing the Word into your heart. Last but not least, listening to bible-based music and movies can indirectly teach you the Word and biblical principles for living.

I have also found it helpful to find a few biblical characters with whom I can identify with. Study what happens to them in their obedience and in their disobedience. Look at the way God sees them in comparison to the way they saw themselves. See how much He loves them unconditionally. This will help you to better relate to God's unconditional love for you.

Once you learn what God requires, you must make a choice to obey Him. This is the choice that will offer you life or death. James 4:17 says that if you know the good you ought to do and do not do it, then you have sinned. Recovery requires obedience to God's instructions for your life. Obedience is turning from independence to dependence on God. It comes easy when your thinking changes from carnal to Christ-like.

Obedience is powerful in the struggle with addiction. It recognizes the presence of an evil being and your power over him. Obedience prevents you from falling victim to Satan. Stay sensitive to God's voice and eager to do His will. You must make a choice to walk in love and unity so that you do not leave a door open for the devil to bring sin into your life. Operate in forgiveness and patience.

Perseverance in obedience guarantees that you will not fall victim to the spirit of addiction again. It offers you complete restoration. God is on your side. He will stand and fight as long as you fight and when you become weak from your long battle, God will fight for you. Either way, the outcome will be victory, over your addiction, over sin, over death.

His sheep know His voice and will follow Him.(John 10:4) Deuteronomy 26:1 says that if you fully obey the Lord and carefully follow all of his commands that

He will set you high above all the nations of the earth.

Successful recovery requires that you walk in obedience. Obedience provides joy and freedom. You are made righteous through obedience.(Romans 5:19) Obedience is keeping God first in your life because you love Him. This love will keep you on target. It will prevent you from yielding to the sin of addiction out of a sincere love for God and an unwillingness to disappoint Him.

MY TRANSFORMATION

_____
_____
_____
_____

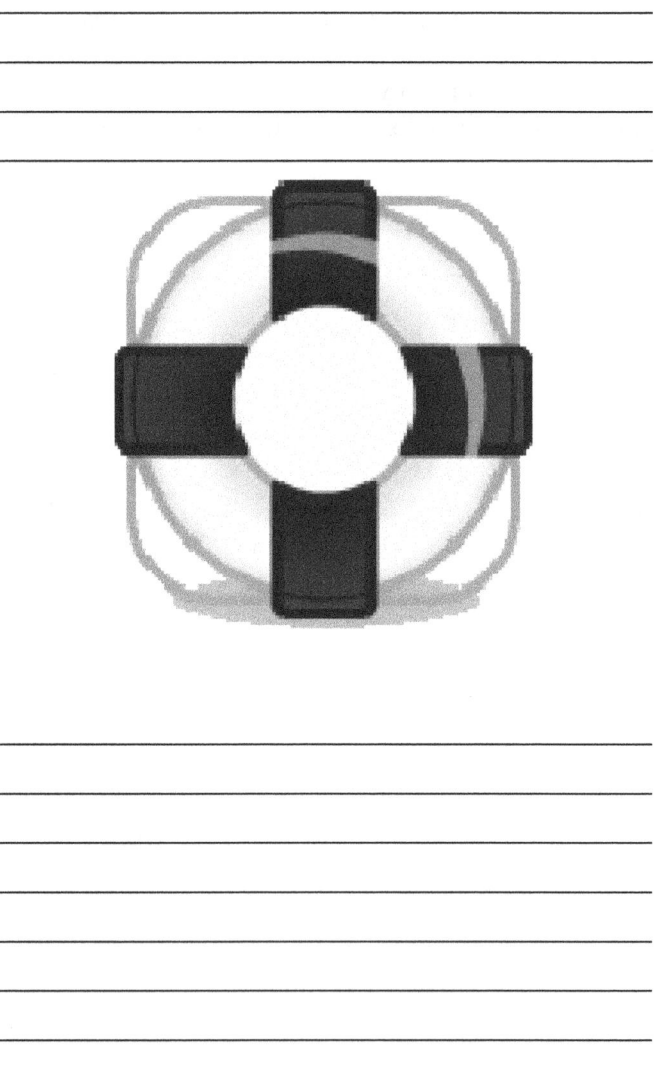

_____
_____
_____
_____
_____
_____
_____

Step 8

Renew Your Mind

> Do not conform any longer to the pattern of this world, but be transformed by the renewing of your mind. Then you will be able to test and approve what God's will is—his good, pleasing and perfect will.
> **Romans 12:2**

Addiction changes the way the brain functions. It conditions your mind to accept wrong thinking, negative thoughts, unwholesome thoughts, sickness, doubt, fear, and failure. It conditions you to sin. Faith in God's promises helps you to recognize the negative thoughts associated with addiction as lies from the enemy. Satan seeks to steal, kill, and destroy.(John 10:10) The Word says that if you resist negative emotions that they will flee from you. Determine that you will maintain a positive attitude regardless of how dark your situation looks. Wrong thinking and negative living steals your victory, the victory that God promises in His Word.

Recovery requires that you make a choice to change. Changing your thinking will change your actions. Looking at things through God's eyes allows you to live as Jesus lived, righteous and holy. Even when you think that no one else knows your thoughts, remember that nothing in all creation is hidden from God's sight. Everything is uncovered and laid bare before the eyes of him to whom we must give account. (Hebrews 4:13) Ask yourself, "If God could see what I was thinking, would I be embarrassed? If your answer is yes, then you need to turn your focus away from

Satan and toward the things of God.

Here's what happens to the renewed mind during God's twelve step program. Your mind will become God-controlled, disciplined, and determined. You will freely accept forgiveness and give forgiveness to those who you believe have harmed you. You will operate in love. You will become thankful-minded, positive, hopeful, focused, and stable. You will receive you victory because His word promises it to you.

Recovery requires a renewing of the mind to the way God intended it to be. It demands that you allow the Holy Spirit to have full control of your thoughts and beliefs. This renewal of the mind requires that you gain an awareness of your words, actions, and deeds that are negative in nature and choose to change. Develop spiritual values and integrity. Spirituality will enrich your life and give you hope and inspiration. Renewing the mind means learning to manage life's daily stresses by alleviating worry. It means allowing God to deal with the challenges that arise. Recovery is resisting negative thoughts. It requires that you only entertain thoughts and actions that line up with the Word of God and that you live with expectancy of the abundant life God promises.

Jesus is always with you. He lives in you and will speak to you when you are willing to listen. Successful recovery requires knowing His voice. He will give you instructions for your life. Listen to them. They will light your path to complete recovery and restoration. The Word requires that you love the Lord with all of your mind.(Matthew 22:37) To do this, your mind must be renewed. It must be trained to think on God's Word. Set your mind on God, His faithfulness, love, mercy, and power.

You are predestined to righteousness. Set your sights on the reward of victory through faith. You have a right to victory because the Lord is victorious. He overcame the world and so can you. Imitate Him in all that you do. Sometimes renewing the mind is as simple as asking yourself, "Would Jesus think what I am thinking? Resist negative thoughts no matter what your circumstances tell you. Train your mind to please Him in every aspect of life. Thinking positive allows you to make positive life changes. It allows you to be led by His spirit and conformed to His image. The more you think like Jesus thinks, the more like Him you will become. As your mind changes so will your life.

Renewing your mind takes reading, meditating, and acting on the Word. Confess God's word and its power over your life. Feed your spirit to keep your flesh under submission. Walk in submission and thanksgiving. Fellowship with other believers. They can speak positive affirmations over you and enrich your life. Forgive yourself and others whom you feel have wronged you. Accept your healing from whatever ails you; your addiction and its physical or emotional effects. Pray daily and at all times in honor and submission to God. Love yourself and others in the love of God. Keep sin, fear and doubt, out of your life. Do not allow it for one moment. Learn to base everything you do on the Word of God. Walk by faith not by sight.(2 Corinthians 2:7) Even if you struggle with sin, confess with your mouth and your heart the things that are of God and your body will come under submission.

No matter what you have been through or who has

hurt you; you have a Father who truly loves you. His spirit lives in you and will change you if you allow Him to. He wants to bless you with the riches of His kingdom. Recovery requires that you recognize the awesome God and Father you serve. He will blot your transgressions away.(Isaiah 43:25) He forgives all sins and gives you a clean slate for reclaiming your life.

Renovating your mind provides the insight necessary to continuously search yourself for weaknesses. It evokes confession of your power over these weakness, though Jesus Christ. The affirmation below will help you through this process.

Overcoming Addiction with Eternal Life Affirmation

I can do all things through Christ who strengthens me. Addiction will not control my life anymore. I am more than a conqueror. My God will supply all of my needs so that I will not look for satisfaction in the world. He is greater than this world and because He lives in me, I am greater than the sin that seeks to destroy me. I will not be afraid, frustrated, depressed, angry, or sick but instead will walk in the love of God knowing that love conquers all.

Romans 8:37; Philippians 4:13; Philippians 4:19; 1 John 4:4; 2 Timothy 1:7

Step 9

Irrevocable Inheritance

> He himself bore our sins in his body on the tree, so that we might die to sin and live for righteousness; by his wounds you have been healed.
> **1 Peter 2:24**

You are the seed of Abraham. That entitles you to a king's inheritance. It has many benefits. Righteousness is just one of your many rights. Your righteousness was guaranteed through the life and death of Jesus. Recovery requires that you choose to walk in the righteousness that Jesus died for you to have. He came to give you abundant life.(John 10:10) God has a plan for your life. But fulfillment of that plan requires determination, perseverance, and faith. Success in life requires that your will desires what God desires. Lay down the selfish destruction of addiction and pick up God's plan for your life.

You don't have to feel worthy to be worthy. Jesus' sacrifice made you worthy, righteous, and whole. Get rid of the stronghold of condemnation. You have a right to be free from the bondage of addiction

Recovery requires that you see yourself the way God sees you and acknowledge God's greatness in you. Acknowledge your ability to do all things through Christ Jesus. Recognize that He is a mighty God who will bless you in proportion to your level of love and obedience to Him. You are created in his likeness and because He created you, you are good. You are unique and have eternal value to God. You hold a high place of privilege. God loves you in spite of your faults. Redemption is yours. He will empower you for success in achieving your goals for life.

You are an ambassador for His kingdom. You are commissioned to bring others to Christ and can only do this if you are living an obedient life of righteousness. Recognize that your weaknesses are made strong in Him. You must love yourself as God loves you and accept yourself because God accepts you.

Understanding your righteousness allows you to see that God is your God and everything He has is yours. If you are pure and upright he will restore you to your rightful place.(Job 8:6) But righteousness requires faith. Faith is the master key to life. Faith will sustain you when everything around you tells you to quit. Refuse to allow doubt, unbelief, and worry to steal your joy. Be patient and allow God to do what He says He will do. He is faithful and just.

Righteousness tells you that victory over addiction is yours. Believe for your recovery and restoration. It is already done.(Luke 1:37) With God, nothing is impossible. Don't allow the enemy to lie to you. He will tell you that you will never regain control over your life or that your addiction will kill you but God offers life. Recognize Satan for what he is, a liar, a deceiver, a murderer.

Your past failures do not determine your present success. God is on your side. Righteousness keeps you focused on your commitment to an addiction-free, sin-free life. Make it a part of your character. Make quality decisions by keeping God first. Stand in obedience with spiritual stamina and endurance knowing that you are entitled to all of the rights of a king. Righteousness gives you the desire to see God's instructions for your life through to fulfillment and work wholeheartedly for the purposes of God.

MY TRANSFORMATION

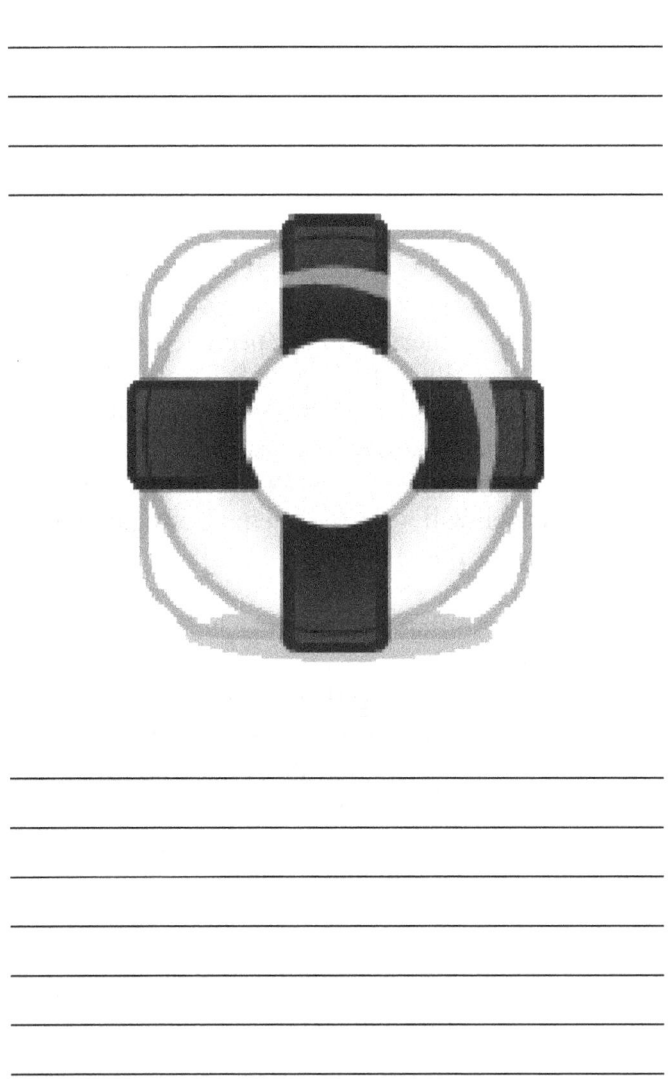

Step 10 — *More Than One Day At A Time*

> For I know the plans I have for you," declares the LORD, "plans to prosper you and not to harm you, plans to give you hope and a future.
> **Jeremiah 29:11**

Receiving your healing and maintaining your deliverance requires that you learn to praise God in all things. Praise manifests God's glory which defeats the enemy and sends him running. It exposes the enemy's lies. It affirms to Satan that you belong to God. It fills your atmosphere with the presence of God and helps you to stay filled the Spirit. Where the Spirit is, evil is not. Addiction or any other sin can not exist where the spirit of the Lord dwells.

Praise is a demon-repellant. Praise brings God's anointing which will keep the enemy from gaining power over your life. It silences the avenger who will come often to try to steal your blessing and elevates your faith level so that you can take hold of the desires of your heart

Recovery requires being thankful at all times and walking joyfully through the trials of life knowing that you have a powerful, faithful, God who loves you and can bring you out of any situation. Praise is the password for entering into God's presence and for receiving victory over whatever binds you, drugs, alcohol, sex, gluttony, etc. It releases the blessings of God. Among them are deliverance, freedom, peace, and restoration. Praise and thanksgiving will help to control your thoughts and keep your mind renewed. Praise allows you to hear from God. It frees His

Righteousness forces you to strive for excellence in all you do.

Jesus healed many sickness; the blind, lame, mute, deaf, and dumb and He can heal 'all' of your sicknesses, as well. Don't think for one second that your sickness is too big for Him. Addiction is no match for the healing power of Jesus. He already paid the price. Lay your pain and sickness at his feet where much healing occurred and still occurs today.

Living past addiction requires evolution through a healing process. Righteousness entitles you to complete healing from your addiction and the results of it. Psalm 107:20 promises that God will heal you and rescue you from the grave. By his stripes you are healed.(Isaiah 53:5) You only need to touch the hem of his garment and have the faith of a mustard seed. Like the woman with an issue of blood, this healing is yours no matter how long you have struggled with addiction.

Despite your ways, God will guide you, comfort you, and restore you.(Isaiah 57:18) He will restore you to health and heal your wounds.(Jeremiah 30:17) If you have been blinded by addiction and sin, he will open your eyes and restore your vision so that you can see everything clearly.(Mark 8:25) If you have been withered away by drugs, alcohol, or any other addiction, Stretch our your heart and He will heal you completely. If you have been paralyzed by sin, take up your bed and walk. God will not only heal you but restore you to your rightful place in Him. In righteousness, God offers complete restoration. The God of all grace, who called you to his eternal glory in Christ, after you have suffered a little while, will himself restore you and make you strong and steadfast.(1 Peter 5:10) The righteous will live forever; not just one day at a time.(Isaiah 51:8)

angels to work on your behalf. It helps you to live in God's grace. It releases miracles, faith, and reminds you of God's goodness.

A life of praise will make recovery for life a reality. Replace your habit with a practice of thanksgiving. Make it a part of your lifestyle. Thank him for the baby steps and see if he doesn't propel you into a place of freedom and righteousness. He will deliver you from whatever binds you. Praise God for whatever you expect to receive from Him. Thank Him in faith for fulfillment of His promises.

Sustaining recovery requires that you never forget the one who delivered you and know that He wants you to live. Living requires recognizing Him as your instructor, your protector, your provider, your counselor; everything you need. He will help you to stand through the trials of life with perseverance and determination. Know yourself enough to know that you are righteous in Christ and that you can overcome whatever the enemy throws in your path. Look at yourself through God's eyes. Through his eyes you will see past your failure to the addiction-free, bondage-free fulfilled life that God has for you.

Never forget that you were created in God's image with His nature. He desires for you to share His vision for your life and to think and act the way He does. You are a winner and will succeed at whatever you do because you were created and pre-destined for greatness. The Lord will sustain you on your sickbed and restore you from your bed of healing. (Psalm 41:3) No matter what your eyes tell you, know that He wants you to have joy, peace, freedom, health, and prosperity; none of which can be achieved in the presence of addiction.

After deliverance from a spirit of addiction, you must choose to live in the support and covering of other believers by finding your place in a local church. Obtaining and maintaining recovery requires that you get rooted in a bible-believing church. This has many benefits. The Word says that one will put a thousand to flight and two will put ten thousand to flight. There is power in numbers. Church membership keeps you surrounded by other believers who will speak Godly blessings into you life. They can pray with you and stand in the gap for you when you become weaken by your trials. Fellow believers can keep you strengthened and encouraged. They can stand in agreement with you for your continued deliverance and restoration. Through them, God will refresh you and keep you built up so that you can withstand the trials that will come during your recovery process. Don't draw back.

Occupy your free time with service to the Lord to prevent idleness and loneliness. Loneliness can bring depression. The enemy will try to use loneliness to convince you that God has forgotten you or that He does not care about you. Draw near to God through His people. He will use them to remind you that you are loved and that you are never alone.

A bible-believing church is a safe place to heal. Many churches offer counseling that can help you to further heal from the hurts that were the catalyst for your addiction.

Fellowshipping with other believers equips you as a saint in God's army to overcome the trials of life. It places you on an unbeatable team where you will learn that you have authority over the power of addiction. This authority is magnified with other believers standing in faith with you.

Church membership teaches you to submit to the authority of others that the Lord has placed in charge of you. Welcome Godly correction and spiritual insight and revelation. The Lord chastises those He loves.(Hebrews 12:6) Fellowshipping will help you to find Godly counsel in the people who have already achieved the success you want. Seek out people who share your struggle and have cleared the path that you are on. They will provide Godly insight into the struggles and the rewards of recovery.

MY TRANSFORMATION

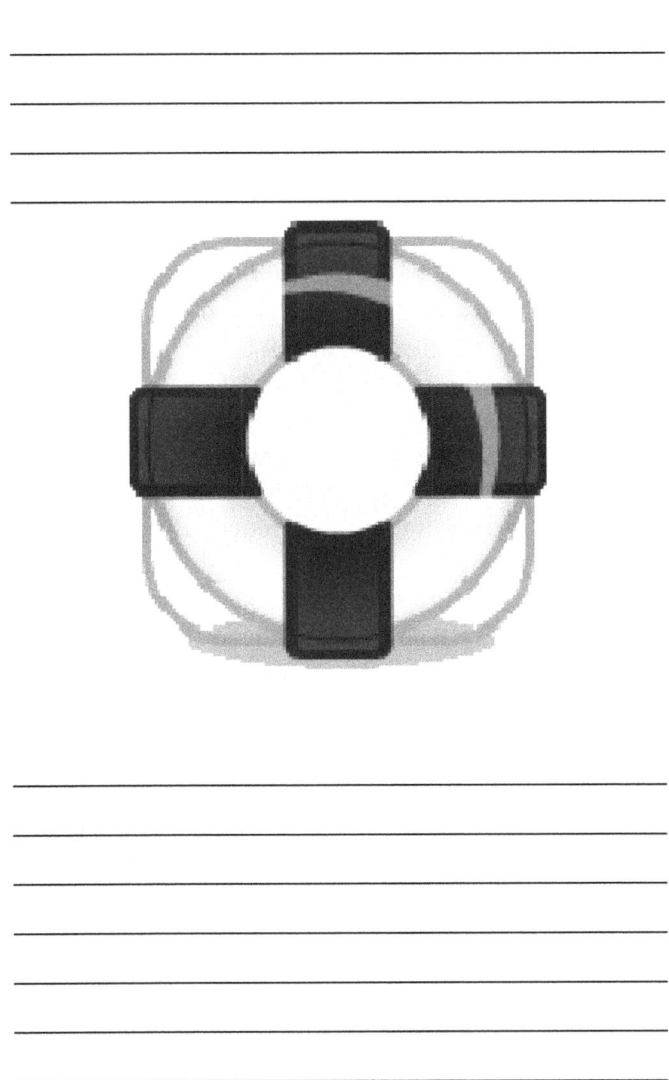

Step 11

Walk by Faith not by Sight

> I have fought the good fight, I have finished the race, I have kept the faith. Now there is in store for me the crown of righteousness, which the Lord, the righteous Judge, will award to me on that day—and not only to me, but also to all who have longed for his appearing
> **2 Timothy 4:7-8**

Recovery requires a life of daily prayer and unwavering faith. Matthew 21:22 says that if you believe, you will receive whatever you ask for in prayer. Prayer is one of the greatest powers God gave to men. It brings results and helps you to overcome the obstacles of life. It is a powerful force against the forces of evil.

Prayer is work. It takes persistence. Prayer takes standing on the Word, refusing to be defeated. It takes an unwavering belief that God will give you the victory over every trial of life, even addiction. Prayer brings the favor of God. In your prayers you will be restored to your righteous state.(Job 33:26)

The Word of God offers very concrete instructions for effective prayer. Matthew 6:6 tells you that when you pray, go into your room, close the door and pray to your Father, who is unseen. Then your Father, who sees what is done in secret, will reward you. Find a quiet place without distraction to pray. Be still and listen for His voice. Wait on the Lord to answer you. Be ready to accept His instructions. Ask specific questions so that you get specific answers. Remember that nothing is too hard for God.

John 14:6 says that the only way to the Father is through the son. John 5:22 says that God has deferred all judgment to the Son. There is power in the name of Jesus. Jesus won your authority and delegated it to you. It is a privilege but you must activate your power. The amount of power you have depends on your faith. Whatever you ask the Father in Jesus name, Jesus will endorse it and God will give it to you. Claim your power, victory, faith, strength, and healing. Use it to overcome the evil in your life. Satan must obey you when you execute your authority through Jesus Christ. Use it.

Faith is believing that all things are possible but the enemy will try to steal this hope. When you believe something to be impossible, Satan will give you all the reasons why it is. If the enemy can cause you to lose faith, he can prevent you from seeing your potential in the Kingdom.

Satan will use guilt and unbelief to prevent progress in your life. Unbelief and guilt brings despair, failure, depression, and destruction. These sinful emotions open the door for negative thoughts and actions. They rob you of God's joy, dull your enthusiasm, and hinder your prayers. They cause you to alienate yourself from others and from God. They can even cause sickness and disease. If allowed to continue, you may soon find yourself walking in disobedience which paralyzes you, cripples your faith, and allows the enemy to keep you right where he wants you; struggling with addiction instead of walking in divine healing and restoration.

Faith is full assurance in Jesus, who is the author and perfector of your faith.(Hebrews 12:2) Faith offers success (2 Chronicles 20:20) and strength (Romans 4:20). It justifies you.(Romans 5:1) Faith allows you to

approach God with freedom and confidence.
(Ephesians 3:12) Faith increases love.(2 Thessalonians 1:4) It brings grace, peace, and eternal life.(Titus 1:4) Faith will shield you from harm.(1 Peter 1:5) It allows you to overcome the world and receive victory. (1 John 5:4)

Faith allows you to release the guilt by cleansing you from a guilty conscience and washes you white a snow.(Hebrews 10:22) It brings victory, peace, joy, and strength.
This is God's will for your life. Successful recovery requires that you use your God-given faith to remove guilt and unbelief from your life. Faith wrecks havoc on the spirit world. It subdues the kingdom of darkness where addiction starts. It allows you to walk in righteousness so that addiction will have no power over your life. Faith obtains the promises of God and stops the lies of the enemy. It gives you victory over all of your enemies by strengthening you in the power of God. It counters any weapon that the enemy tries to use to prevent the fulfillment of God's purpose for your life.

In order to exercise your faith, you must walk in forgiveness. Forgive yourself and those whom you believe have wronged you. Restoration requires that you confess your sin of unbelief and ask for forgiveness. Faith allows you to believe that you will be vindicated. Strive for excellence by using God's grace to help you achieve it. Faith allows you to see the excellence that God sees in you. Vengeance is the Lord's. (Jeremiah 51:6) Remember that only God has the ability to judge. Avoid being judgmental or critical of others. Faith allows you to trust that God is the only true judge and that He will provide justice.

Remember that God loves you even when you make mistakes. Faith allows you to trust Him to love you the way His Word promises He does.

Total faith is evidenced by positive thinking, positive confessions, and positive actions. Recovery requires removing anything that hinders your faith. Stop trying to be like other people or to force your way into a position to which you were not called. Avoid worry, anxiety, apprehension, indecisiveness, hatred, revenge, greed, selfishness, discouragement, or depression. Avoid doubt and unbelief. Think like God thinks. Avoid negative thoughts. Act on God's word and His instructions for your life. Remember your place in Christ, its authority, and its promises.

This position offers freedom from addiction, pain, and sin. During the process of recovery, it is imperative that you take your cares to the Lord. Do not allow emotional stress, worry, anxiety, fear, depression, or any other lie of the enemy to draw you away from the purpose of God. Do not allow the trials of life to push you back into addiction. The Lord promises you healing, health, protection, deliverance, joy, and peace. He promises to provide everything you need. (Philippians 4:19)

Maintaining and sustaining recovery requires putting total belief in the Savior, Jesus Christ. It requires firm and unwavering faith. Faith is never taking eyes off the promises of God. It is never allowing a situation to dominate your thinking or to change what you know God is; everything you need.

Faith is essential for recovery because it allows you to see past your current circumstance to the blessings of God. It helps you to see past tomorrow into eternity. Faith rejects and cast off anything that is contrary to God's Word. It keeps your eyes on eternal things. Walk by the Father's word. Control your thoughts to avoid being oppressed. Faith removes distractions and worry to keep you at peace. Faith is being able to say to the mountain of addiction, "Go throw yourself into the sea" and knowing that because you do not doubt the power of God, the sin of addiction will stop.(Matthew 11:23-24) Faith is believing that you have unlimited access to God and using that access to be what God says you are. It is dreaming big and counting on God to make your dreams a reality; even deliverance from addiction.

MY TRANSFORMATION

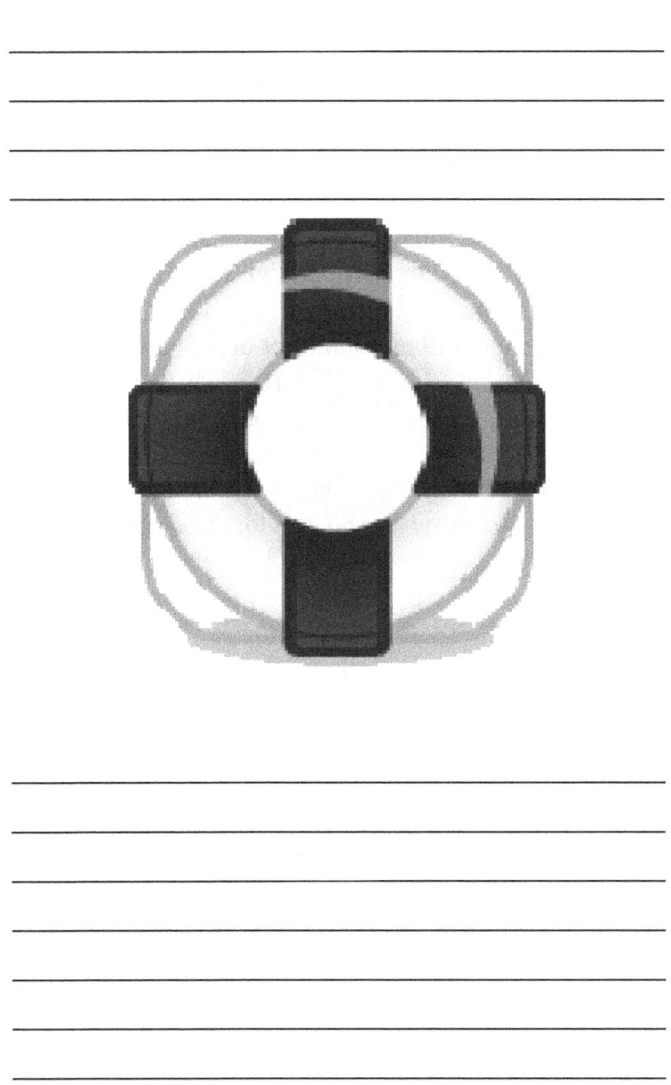

Step 12

Share Your Blessing

> They overcame him by the blood of the
> Lamb and by the word of their testimony;
> they did not love their lives so much as to
> shrink from death.
> **Revelations 12:11**

If someone is caught in a sin, you should restore him gently. (Galatians 6:1) Maintaining deliverance demands that you find ways to be of service to others who may be struggling with addiction. Know that you, through your example, have the ability to release others from the bondage of addiction. Sharing your testimony releases God's light. It brightens your path and the path for others who may be struggling with sin.

Exercise a servant's heart by always being willing to intercede and to stand in the gap for other believers. God will honor your steps to lead others to freedom from bondage. He will sustain you in recovery and spiritual growth.

Opening your heart to others also prevents loneliness. Proverbs 18:24 says that if you show yourselves to be friendly then you will have friends. Loyalty to others encourages them to be loyal. Faithfulness to others encourages them to be faithful. In other words, we will be given whatever we give to others; blessings or curses.

Use your talents, words, and time to help others. Compassion takes your mind off of your own troubles, even the troubles that led you to addiction in the first place. It occupies your life with love for others instead of disappointment in yourself. Find a need and meet it. You will find your own needs being met through your faithful service to others.

Recovery requires that you see and love others the way God sees and loves them. It is required in His Word. Recognize your requirement to cover others in prayer and to stand in the gap for their deliverance and spiritual growth. You are charged with bringing other believers to the saving grace of Christ. It is your assignment. Serving God and others is the master key to unlimited success in your own life. God will honor your attempts to bless others by blessing you.

Fellowship allows you to develop an intimacy with the Lord through your service to Him. It pleases Him. Let your service to God include sharing your testimony with others. He appreciates your obedience to lead others to Him. Keeping the great commission before you will keep sin beneath you. Sharing your story helps you to obtain and maintain your rightful place in the body of Christ and in life.

In All Things Give PRAISE!

Throughout your recovery process, many attacks will come. You will find yourself being condemned about just about everything. But remember that condemnation comes from the Devil. It is evil and evil must be battled in the spirit realm. Prayer is your weapon.

The remainder of this book is a compilation of prayers that will help you through the many trials of life. They can be used in whole or in part. I started creating praise prayers during my trial. I committed them to memory so that in times of need, the word was already sown in my heart. When the enemy came to destroy me, I simply allowed the Holy Spirit to guide my prayers and to pull from my spirit what I needed to persevere.

You must do the same. Remember that we have the authority to drive out evil spirits through Jesus Christ and whatever we bind on earth will be bound in heaven, whatever we loose on earth will be loosed in heaven.(Matthew 10:1 and Matthew 16:9) Use these prayers to sow the word in your heart. Personalize them to your situation. Let praise become a part of you and your prayers. God will make Himself real to you. He will turn your mourning into dancing and your sorrow into joy.

Everyday Battle Prayers

ADDICTION: SMOKING/DRUG ABUSE

Thank you for helping me to stop abusing_____.
I will have no other god before you. You are the only true God. I recognize idolatry as sin and I don't want your wrath to come upon me. My body is your temple. It is sacred because your spirit lives in me. I won't damage or destroy your temple. I realize that I have been bought with a price and that I belong to you. I bind this spirit of addition in Jesus name. Thank you for deliverance from this sin and for restoring me to the wholeness of life that your word promises. Thank you from delivering me from a spirit of addition

Isaiah 44:17
Colossians 3:5
1 Corinthians 8:4
1 Corinthians 3:16
1 Corinthians 6:19
2 Corinthians 6:16

ANGER

Lord, thank you for delivering me from a spirit of anger. I don't want to give the devil a foothold in my life. Thank you for contending with those who contend with me so that I can walk in the forgiveness that your word promises. I trust you to avenge the wrong that has angered me. Thank you for accepting my cry for your mercy and for being faithful in coming to my relief. Thank you for teaching me to do your will, to forgive and accept forgiveness. Create in me a pure heart and renew a steadfast spirit in me. My transgressions are forgiven and my sins no longer count against me. I know that I must forgive others because you have forgiven me. Thank you for helping me to recognize the importance of love to remove the sin of anger. Thank you for teaching me how to be quick to listen, slow to speak, and slow to anger.

Psalm 6
Psalm 32
Psalm 35
Psalm 51
Psalm 58
Ephesians 4:26-27
James 1:19-20
Corinthians 13:8

COMPLAINING

Thank you for delivering me from a complaining spirit. I know that your word demands that I do everything without complaining and arguing. I want to be blameless and pure. I want to be able to boast on the day of Christ that I did not run or labor in vain. I will be content with what I have because I know that you will never leave me or forsake me. I say with confidence, You are my helper. Thank you for making all things work for my ultimate good.

Philippians 2:14
Hebrews 13:5-6

CONTROLLING YOUR TONGUE

Thank you for helping me not to sin with my mouth. I know that spreading slander makes me a fool. My tongue is choice silver and can nourish many; my mouth a fountain of life. I don't want to come to ruin by being a chattering fool. I want to honor you with my actions as well as my words. I know that if I control what I say that I can keep my whole body in check and that I have the power of life and death in my tongue. I choose life and I want to offer others life through the things I say.

Psalm 39:1
Proverbs 10
Proverbs 18:21
Matthew 15:8
James 3:2

DELIVERANCE

Thank you for my deliverance from_____.
I recognize this sin as a destructive force at work. I bind the spirit of _____, right now, in Jesus name. You are my place of shelter as I escape Satan's attempts to destroy me. Thank you for protecting my heart from anguish and my soul from destruction. Thank you for confusing the wicked and snatching me from the grasp of the enemy. Your unfailing kindness has given me victory over the powers of darkness.

Psalm 18:49
Psalm 54

DEPRESSION

Lord, your word tells me that I will have troubles but it also promises to deliver me from them all. With you, everything will work for my ultimate good. Thank you for setting my feet on your solid ground. I will not be afraid or discouraged. I will wait patiently for you. Lord, I know that you go before me in my struggles and are always with me. Your word says that you are close to the brokenhearted and will save those who are crushed in spirit. Thank you for your compassion which comforts me. Thank you for pouring out your love on me when I need it the most and for delivering me from all of my troubles. Thank you for turning my mourning into dancing.

Deuteronomy 31:8
Psalm 34:18
Psalm 40:1-3
Isaiah 49:13
Romans 5:5

DISCOURAGEMENT

Lord, thank you for helping me to be strong and courageous. I will not be afraid because I know that you are with me. My hope is in you. I won't let my heart be troubled because I trust that you will never leave me or forsake me. Thank you for sustaining me according to your promise and reviving my heart and spirit. Even when things seem overwhelming, I know that nothing is too hard for you. Thank you for giving me the confidence I need to persevere. Thank you for lifting my heavy burdens and freeing me up to live the joyous life you have for me.

Deuteronomy 31:6
Psalm 119:116
Isaiah 57:15
Jeremiah 32:17
John 14:1-2
Hebrews 10:35

DISOBEDIENCE/SIN

I come before your throne of grace in my time of need so that temptation cannot seize me. Here I find confidence, grace, and mercy in you. Lord, I love you and I want to show you by obeying your commands. I am your disciple and I will hold onto your truth. I will not depart from the words of your lips. I know that you will reward each person according to what he has done. I want to earn a great reward. I know that it is not you tempting me but an evil being and I bind this spirit of _____ in Jesus name. I know that Satan is prowling around like a roaring lion looking to devour me. Thank you for helping me to remain obedient to your word and to escape the grasp of the enemy.

Job 23:12
Matthew 16:27
John 8:31-32
John 14:23
1 Corinthians 10:13
Hebrews 4:16
James 1:2-3, 13-14
1 Peter 5:8-10

DIVORCE

Thank you for taking away thoughts of divorce from me. I recognize this as a tactic of the enemy for the destruction of God's family. I will not let evil separate what you have put together, me and my spouse as one flesh. I know that divorce is not your will for my marriage. I will not allow my heart to be hardened towards my spouse and I will walk in forgiveness and love. I will fulfill my marital duty to my spouse and retain the place in life to which I have been called. Maintaining the ministry of my marriage is a part of that calling. I cast my cares on you, knowing that you care for me and my spouse and that you will preserve our marriage for your purpose.

Matthew 19:3-12
Mark 10:2-12
1 Corinthians 7

DOMESTIC VIOLENCE

Thank you for delivering me from this spirit of abuse that seeks to destroy me. I recognize abuse as sin and I rebuke this evil spirit of abuse in Jesus name. Your word tells me that the wages of sin is death. I will live and not die. I will have life more abundantly. Thank you for deliverance and restoration to righteousness. I will be slow to anger, abounding in love and faithfulness. Help my victim to be restored to wholeness. Thank you for pouring out your love and forgiveness on me when I need it the most. Thank you for guarding my heart and mind and for giving me a peace that transcends all understanding.

Exodus 34:6b
Luke 17:3
Romans 6:23
Philippians 4:7

FAITH

Lord, thank you for giving me the faith to stand in the face of adversity. I praise you for your faithfulness. I trust you with my whole heart and I will not lean not on my own understanding. I acknowledge you in all my ways and I thank you for making my path straight I have received the strict training offered in your word and I want to receive a prize that glorifies you, a crown that will last forever. Thank you for helping me to run this race with persistence and complete assurance in you.

Proverbs 3:5-6
2 Corinthian 9:24-25

FAILURE

Thank you for delivering me from a spirit of insecurity. I will be am strong and courageous. I will not be terrified or discouraged because I know that you are with me wherever I go. I recognize that all have sinned and come short of the glory of God but that there is no condemnation in you. I am justified freely by your grace. I am redeemed through Jesus Christ. I will be confident knowing that confidence is richly rewarded. I will persevere. I can do all things through you who strengthen me. I am more than a conqueror.

Joshua 1:9
Romans 3:23-24
Philippians 4:13
Hebrews 10:35-36

FEAR

Thank you for delivering me from a spirit of fear. I walk through this shadow of death without fear because I know that you are with me. I trust you to keep me safe and I thank your help in this time of need. I will not be dismayed because my mind is in perfect peace. Thank you for the strength to endure. I am more than a conqueror because you love me. I am not afraid, man can do nothing to me. Greater are you who is in me than he who is in the world.

Isaiah 23:3
Isaiah 35:4
Isaiah 41:10
Psalms 4:8
Psalms 23:4
Proverbs 29:25
Romans 8:37
Hebrews 13:6

FORGIVENESS

Lord, I confess my sin of _____ right now and I thank you for your forgiveness. Thank you for hearing my cries and for opposing those who contend with me so that I can walk in the forgiveness that your word promises. Thank you for your faithfulness and compassion. Thank you for blotting out my transgressions. My soul rejoices and delights in your salvation. Thank you for creating in me a pure heart and for renewing a steadfast spirit in me. I am blessed because my transgressions are forgiven; my sins no longer count against me. Thank you for being my hiding place and for protecting me from condemnation. Thank you for teaching me to do your will, to forgive and accept forgiveness.

Psalm 6
Psalm 32
Psalm 35
Psalm 51
Psalm 58

FORNICATION

I recognize fornication as sin. I realize that this deceiving spirit of fornication comes from a hypocritical liar, Satan. I would rather lose the part of my body that causes me to sin than to send my whole body to hell. I bind this spirit of fornication, right now, in Jesus name. I know that my members are part of Christ himself and I recognize that my body is the temple of the holy spirit. It was bought with a price. I will honor you with every area of my body by living right. I am devoted to you and I want to please you. I know that everything you created is good. That includes me. I will live righteous because I am righteous through you. Thank you for delivering me from a spirit of sexual impurity.

Matthew 5:28-30
1 Corinthians 6:15-20
1 Corinthians 7:32-40
1 Timothy 4:1-8

GOSSIPING/BACKBITING

Thank you for helping me to stop judging others because I don't want to be unjustly judged. I realize that I might have a plank in my own eye therefore I have no room to look at the speck in my brother's eye. I am not a hypocrite and I won't grieve your Holy Spirit by speaking against my brother and your law. I know that you are the only Lawgiver and Judge. I will be obedient to your word by keeping unwholesome talk from coming out of my mouth. I will be kind, compassionate, and forgiving, just as Christ forgave me. Thank you for showing me how to build others up according to their needs. Thank you for helping me to take off my old self and it's practices and put on a new self which is in the image of the you.

Matthew 7:1-5
Ephesians 4:29
Colossians 3:10
James 4:11

GREED

I recognize that greed is sin and I bind this evil spirit in Jesus name. Greed is idolatry and I will have no other god before you, not even money. I will not operate in extortion or take pride in stolen goods. I realize that all of the things that I accumulate here on earth are meaningless in heaven and that my life does not consist in the abundance of my possessions. I will not let this spirit of greed steal my harvest. I will sow generously into your kingdom knowing that I will reap a generous reward. I won't rob you of what is yours. I trust you to provide all that I need. I know that if I am greedy then the love of God cannot be in me and I want you to be with me always. I know that it is up to me to allow you to stay by being honest and righteous in my dealings. Thank you for delivering me from a spirit of greed. Nothing shall separate me from you.

Psalm 62:10
Ecclesiastes 2:11
Luke 12:15
2 Corinthians 9:6-8
Ephesians 5:3-7
John 3:17

GRIEF

Thank you for delivering me from a spirit of grief. I know that you are close to me, even in my despair. I know that death is a part of life. Your word tells me that grief is for people who have no hope. My hope is in You Lord. I believe that Jesus died and rose so that my loved one, who died in Jesus, is in heaven. I know that my grief will be turned to joy. My comfort in my suffering is in your promise. It preserves my life. Your unfailing love is my comfort.

Psalm 119:50,76
1 Thessalonians 4:13-14
Psalm 34:18
John 16:20

GUIDANCE

Your word says that you guide the humble in what is right and teach them the way to go. I lift my soul to you in trust. My hope is in you. I know that you hear my cries for help and that you are with me. Probe and examine me to make sure that I remain on your narrow path. I know that by your hand I am saved from harm and all things will work for my ultimate good. You are my refuge and my rock. Remove anything that is not of you from me. I will not sin with my mouth and will keep myself from evil. Thank you for making me the apple of your eye. Thank you for leading me in your righteousness and making my paths straight. Thank you for lighting my path and showing me the way.

Psalm 5
Psalm 17
Psalm 25
Psalm 31

GUILT

Thank you for delivering me from a spirit of guilt. I know that you heard my cry because you have set me free from the condemnation of the devil. I know that if you kept a record of sins then no one could stand. Thank you for your forgiveness. I receive it right now. I am blessed to have been washed, sanctified, and justified through you. I am not discouraged because through you, I find faith, confidence, and freedom. My hope is unwavering because I know that you are faithful. Thank you for sprinkling my heart with sincerity and cleansing me from a guilty conscience.

Psalm 130:3-4
Ephesians 3:12
Romans 8:1-2
1 Corinthians 6:11
Hebrews 10:22-23

HEALING

Lord, thank you for my healing. Thank you for taking up my infirmities, carrying my disease, and giving me peace. I have walked through the valley of the shadow of death but I don't fear this evil. I know that you are with me. I confess any sin in my life and ask for forgiveness right now. Thank you for restoring comfort to me and guiding me through this trial. I recognize that this trial is only temporary, it will pass. I am more than a conqueror because you love me.

Psalm 23:4
Isaiah 57:18
Matthew 8:17
John 16:33
Roman 8:37

HOMOSEXUALITY

Thank you for delivering me from a spirit of sexual impurity. I will stop disgracing my body because I understand that homosexuality is an abomination. I won't accept this lie of the enemy as your truth. I recognize this trap of the enemy as sinful lust and I rebuke it in Jesus name right now. I realize that if I continue this indecent act that I will receive a due penalty for my perversion. Knowing that the wages of sin is death, I chose life through you. Thank for coming to live inside of this temple and show me how to live a righteous life that is pleasing to you.

Romans 1:24-27

HOPELESSNESS

Thank you for removing the spirit of hopelessness from me. I recognize this feeling as destructive forces at work. I rebuke them in Jesus name right now. In my distress I call on you and I know that you hear my voice. My heart is glad and my tongue will rejoice; my hope is in you. I rest assured in you. Thank you for your mercy and your counsel which guide my life. Because of it, I will walk in your truth and let you light and your truth guide me. Thank you for forgiveness, redemption, and restoration.

Psalm 18:6
Psalm 39:7
Psalm 43:3
Psalm 55:11
Psalm 73:24-26
Psalm 86:2

HYPOCRISY

Thank you for delivering me from a spirit of hypocrisy. I won't let my worship be in vain. I will live what I preach. I am beautifully made in your image and I want to walk in obedience as an example of Your existence in me. When others see me, they will desire to serve you. I will honor you with my heart as well as my lips. I will light the path for others to come to know you by being an example of your righteousness and by being obedient to your word. I will not neglect the more important matters of the law; justice, mercy, and faithfulness. Thank you for showing me the importance of my actions matching the condition of my heart.

Matthew 15:7-9
Matthew 23

IMPATIENCE

Lord, thank you for delivering me from a spirit of impatience. I will be still and wait patiently on you. I know that you are not a man who would lie. I will stand firm on your promises. Just as you have shown me grace and mercy. Let me show this same mercy to others. I know that though patience that I will inherit the promise. I know that you are in control and that all things will work for my ultimate good. Thank you for helping to share in your glory, honor, and peace by being strong you.

Psalm 27:13-14
Psalm 37:7
Psalm 40:1
Romans 2:7
James 5:7-8 1
Timothy 1:16
Hebrew 6:12

INFERTILITY

I know that you have the ability to open the womb of the righteous. You did it for Hannah, Leah, and Rachel and I know that you can help me because you have the ability to bless the womb of women. Thank you for taking this barren women and making me a mother of children. Thank you for increasing my numbers. Thank you for blessing the fruit of my womb. I know that children are a reward from the Lord. I thank you for this reward right now. Thank you for unwavering faith that allows me to see past my circumstance to your promise. In Jesus name, I call those things that are not as though they are so.

Genesis 29:31
Genesis 30:22
Genesis 49:25
Deuteronomy 7:13
Psalm 113:9
Psalms 127:3
Romans 4:17
Romans 20

INSECURITY

Thank you for delivering me from spirit of insecurity. I know that I am created in your image. I am beautifully made. I will be sober in my judgment of myself and will think of myself with the measures of faith that you have given me. Thank you for allowing your righteous right hand to guide and help me. I know that because you are for me, that no one can be against me. I am confident in your power. Thanks you for helping me by removing the fear that controls me. I find refuge in you knowing that you live in me therefore I am righteous through Christ Jesus and no weapon forged against me will prosper.

Genesis 1:27
Psalm 34:22
Romans: 3-5
1 John 4:15-16

JEALOUSY

Thank you for delivering me from a spirit of jealousy. I will not be envious of my neighbor because I know that envy, bitterness, and covetousness is not of you. I bind this spirit and its attempts to destroy me in Jesus name. I know that what I have here on earth means nothing and that I cannot take it with him when I die. Instead, I want to be rich in you. Thank you for showing me how to store up treasures in heaven by being obedient to our word.

Galatians 5:19
James 3:14-16
Psalm 49:16-17

LAZINESS

Thank you for delivering me from spirit of laziness. I want to store up provision and gather a harvest. I won't live in poverty. I know that lazy hands make a poor and that if I don't work that I won't eat or have the things that I need. I want diligent hands that will bring about wealth; not just on here on earth but in heaven. I will make the most of every opportunity to walk out my salvation with my will and my actions so that I can be used for your purpose. My ambition will win the respect of others so that they will desire to come to know you.

Proverbs 6:6-11
Proverbs 10:4-5
Ephesians 5:15
Philippians 2:12-13
1 Thessalonians 4:11-12
2 Thessalonians 3:6-15

LUST

Thank you for removing lust from my heart and protecting me from the deceiver, Satan, who seeks to destroy me. I bind this deceiving spirit right now in Jesus name. Thank you for purging my mind and body so that I can see clearly that my body belongs to my husband/wife, alone. Thank you for sanctifying me so that I will avoid sexual immorality. I don't want my right eye nor my right hand to cause me to sin. I would rather lose that part of my body than for my entire body to go to hell. I will control my mind and my body so that it will be kept holy and honorable and my temple will be pleasing to you.

1 James 1:13-14
Matthew 5:29-30
Deuteronomy 22:24
Proverbs 6:25
1 Corinthians 7:4
1 Thessalonians 4:3-5

LYING

Thank you for delivering me from a lying spirit. I recognize this as sin and I bind this spirit in Jesus name. I know that if I continue to lie that I will be punished. I am not wicked or unclean and I will not give a false report. I don't want to be a club, sword, or sharp arrow aimed at hurting other people. Thank you for purging this evil from me. I will watch my ways and keep my tongue from sin. I am wise and my lips of truth and righteousness will nourish many. I will control my tongue so that I can control my whole body. I will not delight in evil but rejoice in truth.

Exodus 23:1
Deuteronomy 19:19
Proverbs 19:9
Proverbs 25:18
Matthew 15:19
Psalm 39:1
Proverbs 10:18-21
James 3:1-12
1 Corinthians 13:6

MASTURBATION

I recognize masturbation as sin. I would rather lose the part of my body that causes me to sin than to send my whole body to hell. I recognize that my body is the temple of the holy spirit and that my members are part of Christ himself. I was bought with a price. I will honor God with every area of my body and my actions will be pleasing you. I am devoted to you in body and spirit. I will not follow these deceiving spirits. I know that they come from a hypocritical liar, Satan and I rebuke his power over me right now, in Jesus name. I recognize that obedience and righteousness holds promise for this life and life to come. Thank you for giving me the integrity and uprightness that will preserve me.

Matthew 5:28-30
1 Corinthians 6:15-20
1 Corinthians 7:32-40
1 Timothy 4:1-8
Psalm 25:21

OBESITY

Thank you for removing the spirit of gluttony from me. I know that it can/has led to obesity which puts my life in jeopardy. Thank you from delivering me from this spirit of addition. Idolatry is sin and I will have no other idol before you, not even food. My body is sacred and your spirit lives in me. I will not damage or destroy your temple. I have been bought with a price and I belong to you. I will separate myself from this sin because I know that there is no agreement between you and obesity/gluttony. Thank you for this wonderfully made temple of the Holy Spirit and I will not let gluttony destroy it.

Isaiah 44:17
1 Corinthians 8:4
Colossians 3:5
1 Corinthians 3:16
1 Corinthians 6:19
2 Corinthians 6:16
Psalm 139:14-16

PEACE

Thank you for giving me peace about_____.
I will not be troubled or afraid. You are my Prince of Peace. Thank you allowing your grace to keep me. I am safe and secure because you love me. Thank you for enlarging me and increasing my joy. Thank you for sending the Holy Spirit to teach me and remind me of your word and for leaving your peace with me. I am justified through faith and through your blood. Thank you for reconciliation, for guarding my heart and mind, and for a peace that transcends all understanding.

Numbers 6:24-26
Psalm 122:6
Isaiah 9:2, 7
John 14:25-27
Romans 5:1,9,11
Philippians 4:7

PHYSICAL PAIN

I know that pain is a tactic used by Satan to torment me and I rebuke his attempts in the name of Jesus. Lord, thank you for being strong when I am weak. Even righteous men have troubles but I trust you to deliver me from them all, including this pain. I am a joint heir to your kingdom and I share in your suffering so that I may share in your glory. This pain will not control me. It is only a trial and I will rejoice as your glory is revealed. Thank you for your sufficient grace that helps me to persevere. Thank you for healing me of the physical pain in my body and helping me to receive that eternal glory that far outweighs these momentary troubles.

1 Peter 2:20
1 Peter 4:12-13
Psalms 34:19
Mark 14:36
Romans 8:17-18
1 Corinthians 4:17
1 Corinthians 12:7-10

PRIDE

Thank you for delivering me from a spirit of pride. I know that you hate pride and arrogance and I don't want to be cursed, disgraced, or rebuked. I want to remain in you loving care forever. I will use sound judgment in my speech and actions and walk in humility because your word says that with humility comes wisdom and wisdom is better than gold. Thank you for removing pride, selfishness, and vanity from my life and helping me to avoid destruction. Thank you for giving me prudent understanding and power so that I can be sober in my judgment according to the measure of faith that you have given me. Thank you for helping me to be tender and compassionate like you.

Psalm 119:21
Proverbs 8:13
Proverbs 11:2
Proverbs 16:18
Proverbs 8:12-14
Romans 12:3
Philippians 2:1-5

PROFANITY

Thank you for helping me to stop using profanity. I know that profanity is displeasing to you and I recognize it as a foot hold that can become a stronghold if allowed to continue. I don't want to give the devil power in my life. I bind this cursing spirit in the name of Jesus. Thank you for avenging the wrong that has angered me so that I don't sin in my anger. Thank you for teaching me how to be quick to listen, slow to speak, and slow to anger and for helping me to recognize the importance of love to remove the sin of anger. I will not let unwholesome talk come out of my mouth. I will speak only what is helpful for building up others and is beneficial to all those who are listening.

Ephesians 4:26-27
James 1:19-20
1 Corinthians 13:8
Ephesians 4:29

PROTECTION

Thank you for protection from the enemy's snare. My trust is in you. You have delivered me, time after time therefore, I know that you are faithful. Thank you for rest in the shelter of in your shadow. No harm will come near me. Thank you for being my refuge and my fortress in this time of trouble.

Psalm 22:4
Psalm 91:1-2

STEALING

Thank you for delivering me from a spirit of greed. I know that your word tells me not to steal and that stealing is sin. I understand that the wages of sin is death and I do not want to die. I choose life through obedience to your word. I will store up my treasures in heaven where moth and rust cannot destroy them. Thank you for abundance and prosperity so that I no longer have the desire to steal. Thank you that I am no longer the thief who steals other peoples treasures and for helping me to be the person showing others how to store up treasures in heaven for themselves.

Exodus 20:15
Matthew 6:19
John 10:10
Ephesians 4:28
Romans 6:23
Psalms 132:15

STEWARDSHIP

Thank you for helping me to be a good steward over all that you have given me. I will be a faithful and wise manager because I recognize that a good steward will be rewarded. I will use them with prudence in accordance to your word. I will not be quick-tempered, violent, or dishonest in my attempts to obtain prosperity. I want to be an overseer of your possessions and be entrusted with your work. Thank you for abundance, for trusting me with all of your possessions, and giving me power over the spirit of poverty.

Matthew 25:29
Matthew 20:8
Luke 12:42
Luke 16:1-3
Titus 1:7

STRENGTH

Thank you for strengthening me through this trial. I will not be fearful or dismayed. I will not be perplexed, abandoned, struck down, nor destroyed. I know that because you are my God, that I will be upheld with your righteous right hand. Thank you Holy Spirit for interceding on my behalf. I know that your grace is sufficient for me and that your power is made perfect in my weakness. Thank you for keeping me strong and blameless until the end.

Isaiah 41:10
Romans 8:26
1 Corinthians 1:8
2 Corinthians 4:8
2 Corinthians 12:9-10

TITHES/OFFERING

Thank you for helping me to be obedient to your word by showing me the importance of tithes and offerings. I love you so much and I want to show you by excelling in the grace of giving. I know that your son, Jesus, though he was rich became poor so that through his poverty I might be rich. Thank you for supplying seed for the sower. I will sow generously with the expectation of reaping a generous reward. I will be willing, eager, and cheerful in my giving. My giving is in thanksgiving for all you have done for me. Thank you for supplying everything I need so that there is no lack in my life and so that I have abundance to sow into your kingdom.

2 Corinthians 8:7-12
2 Corinthians 9:6-11

UNFORGIVENESS

Thank you for delivering me from a spirit of unforgiveness. I forgive my brother who has sinned against me. I will obey your mandates because I love you and want to please you. I refuse to live with the torment of unforgiveness. I will love my neighbor and my enemies. and pray for those who persecute me. Thank you for giving me relief from my distress. I will dwell in a place of peace and keep my heart pure. I know that love keeps no record of wrong doings. I will operate in love because you, who are love, lives in me. I don't want to miss your grace. I don't want a bitter root to grow up, cause trouble or defile me.

Matthew 18:21-35
Matthew 5:43-48
Judges 6:3
Psalm 4:1
Psalm 73:1
1 Corinthians 13:5
Ephesians 5:1
Hebrew 12:14-15

WORRY/ANXIETY

Thank you for providing everything that I need so that I don't need to worry. I know that I am more valuable than the birds and you provide so completely for them. Therefore, I know that you will provide everything I need. I will cast all my cares on you because I know that you care for me. Thank you for guarding my heart and mind and not allowing me to be anxious about anything. I thankfully present my request to you. Thank you for your peace that transcends all understanding.

Matthew 6:25-27
Philippians 4:6
1 Peter 5:7

TRANSFORMED!!!

_____
_____
_____
_____

_____
_____
_____
_____
_____
_____
_____
_____

www.ingramcontent.com/pod-product-compliance
Lightning Source LLC
Chambersburg PA
CBHW071722040426
42446CB00011B/2182